THE GAME

Credit 101

Torrie Blackmon

THE GAME

Book and Cover design by Torrie Blackmon

First Edition: Month 2020

*Cleaning Credit

First and foremost, what is credit? The ability of a customer to obtain goods or services before payment, based on the trust that payments will be made in the future. This is what every person needs in order to move forward in the real world. Understanding how important credit is will help guide you to a better life style. Learning what your Fico score is and why it is used is very important too. FICO aka your middle score is what lenders use to evaluate your credit worthiness. There are so many different ways to access your FICO® scores for free; Try contacting your credit card company or bank to receive a free monthly FICO score.

There are tons of credit repair companies; But why pay hundreds or thousands of dollars when you can do it yourself for free. The only thing you will need is this book and a little bit of patience. First things first you have to know where you are, in order to know where you're headed. Find out everything that's listed on your credit report by using the website www.annualcreditreport.com. This is a free website, but can only be used once a year. So make sure you save every important detail.

During this time of cleaning, never apply for new credit. Never have your name ran for any type of inquiry; As this will dirty up your credit again. Once you obtain the free credit report, dispute any errors you may find by writing a sample letter to each credit bureaus. Make sure to send in proof of identity such as bank statement's and I'd's all with the same address.

Any inquiries that are two years or older you may want to dispute; Including any incorrect addresses. Once you have sent these documents to each bureau using certified mail they will give you a written response within the next 30 days. Word to the wise, if you are not at fault <u>Dispute It</u>! This applies to anything such as late payments, account errors and identity errors. Boosting your credit score after it is cleaned is another trick of the trade.

Now let's talk about Trade-lines. Trade-lines also known as Trades, are lines of credit that the borrower has held open in good standing for a long period of time, typically at least 2 years. They are often associated with authorized users being added in order to gain **a credit** increase. These trades can help boost your score upward to 100 points or more. Trades can be purchased and applied using independent authorized companies such as

https://superiortradelines.com/facts/add-tradelines-to-your-credit-report/.

Be sure to gather as much information as needed before applying for new trade lines.

*Overcome debt & Build credit

Now that you have fixed a few glitches on your credit report, it's now time to overcome debt and build credit. One of the world's top debt is acquired from credit cards. Never think that a credit card with a balance as small as $200 won't do any harm! In fact, it's very harmful than you can imagine. Never use a credit card to cover your spending habits. Once you max your credit card out, the credit bureau is notified and your score will take a drastic hit.

Always divide by 3 while using your credit card. By taking your max limit and divide by 3 you will create your "Real" limit. No matter how much you may need fast cash, never go over your new limit. Continue to make all payments on time. By doing this, you will gain additional points to your score. Your value to financial institutions will look phenomenal over time!

Fun Fact: 3 is a fun number in the credit world. Every three months that you maintain a perfect credit card balance with zero late payments you can contact the credit card company and ask for a credit increase. This will increase the limit of your card, while also increasing your credit score.

*Collections

You have come across a speed bump in the credit road. Not paying on your accounts and skipping bill payments have damaged your name. This is called delinquencies; which is the failure to pay an outstanding debt. This is the worst thing that can possibly affect your credit score. For example, your credit score can drop as much as 100 points after numerous missed payments being applied to your credit report. Not only that, these delinquencies can stay on your report for a total of seven years.

Something as small as a 30-day late payment on your car note can stick to your credit history for seven long years, Yikes! The way around delinquencies is to always pay your Bill's on time. If you can't afford it, don't get it! In case you do acquire a delinquency it's not the end of the world. There are a few tips to overcome that threshold. The first is by requesting a goodwill adjustment from the original creditor to remove the layers payments. Second, negotiate removals by offering to sign up for automatic payments directly from your bank card. Last but not least, dispute any late payments that may look inaccurate to you.

Fun Fact: Never, never pay a delinquency that has already been sold to a 3rd party and applied to your credit. This is called a charge off by the original debt owner. For example, you owe a past due phone bill to XYZ Telecommunications and you fail to pay them; This now will result in a delinquency. Now you have an unknown company called ABC Collections contacting you about the balance owed. What have happened is XYZ Telecommunications have sold the account to ABC Collections to recoup some of the losses. In return ABC Collections will buy the past due account for a small fee and try to make a profit by contacting you to pay the past due debt. But remember even if you pay the past due balance, the delinquent account will still remain on your credit report. "Read this twice because it gets kind of tricky".

*Reaping the benefits

You're now winning the game! Establishing good credit has landed you in the elite club. There are several things you can now benefit from by maintaining good credit. You can now get loans with lower interests rates.

An interest rate is the percentage of principal charged by the lender for the use of its money. The interest can cost a borrower thousands of dollars if they are not careful. The higher the credit score the lower the interest percentage you will pay.

You can now get approved for higher limits on money borrowed as well. With a good score banks are more willing to offer you more money with more time to pay it back. Living arrangements are now easier than ever. You can now get approved for better apartments and homes. Most landlords ask for credit scores while renting to tenants. You now have a better score that shows you are more responsible than your counterparts. This giving you the upper hand over other applicants.

*Creating wealth using real estate

There is power In ownership. Now that your credit is good and you have buying power, let's leverage this credit to build wealth. Moving from renting to owning is a perfect step. Real estate will always appreciate with time, so start early.

Every human being on the planet Earth will need a place to live, this is the exact reason why real estate is so important. Start off by researching banks and apply for a mortgage. You will need an acceptable income with a minimal debt ratio. Hold off on any major purchases such as vehicles or new credit cards because this will increase your debt ratio. A higher debt ratio will result in less money approved by the bank or even a rejection.

Banks will request two years of prior tax returns to prove your living stability. Once the bank sends out an approval letter with the spending limit you are all set to start searching for hour new home. Be on the lookout for 1st time homeowner credits and new buyer programs. These programs can be very beneficial to the purchaser, they may even allow the purchaser to avoid a down payment altogether.

Fun fact: Never over spend or make extravagant purchases. You will want to keep a set balance so that you can later apply for a 2nd rental property if that option may arise. Remember, a low debt ratio can be helpful with being credited with more money later down the road. Become the Landlord! This is where you start to gain wealth.

Acknowledgements:

The final outcome of this book required a lot of guidance and assistance from many people and I am extremely privileged to have got this all along the completion of my project. All that I have done is only due to such supervision and assistance and I would not forget to thank my supporters.

Credit Bureau Letter

[Your Name]
[Address]
[City, State, Zip]
[Phone Number]

[Date of Letter]

[Credit Bureau Agency]
[Address]
[City, State, Zip]

Re: [Account Number]

In reviewing the attached credit bureau report issued by your agency, I have discovered an error. The following account is reported inaccurately:

Company Name: ____

Account Number: ____

Under the provisions of the 1977 Federal Fair Credit Reporting Act, I hereby request that your agency prove to me in writing the accuracy of the reporting of this account. Under the terms of the Act and succeeding court cases, you have thirty days to prove to me the accuracy or you must remove the account from my Credit Report. I am asking that you do so.

This letter was sent by Certified Mail with a return receipt requested. I am expecting a response within thirty days. If I do not hear from you promptly, I will follow up with whatever action that is necessary to cause my report to be corrected.

Please feel free to call me with any question you may have at the above phone number.

Sincerely,
[Sign here]

[Your Typed Name]

No Response Regarding Disputed Information After 30 Days-- Equifax

[Date]

Equifax
Disclosure Department
PO Box 740241
Atlanta, GA 30374

RE: [Your name]

        [Your current address]

        Previous address:

        Social Security number:

        Date of Birth:

To Whom It May Concern:

Over thirty days ago, I wrote to your company indicating my dispute of information in my credit report. A copy of my original letter accompanies this correspondence. As of today's date, Equifax has not responded to my dispute and therefore must remove from my credit file all information disputed in my correspondence.

Under the Fair Credit Reporting Act, your bureau was to have completed its reinvestigation of disputed information within 30 days. This 30-day mark has come and gone without any response from your office.

I am requesting your assistance in the verification of the removal of the disputed data from my credit report. Please send to my address provided above an updated credit report at no cost to me as proof that these items have been removed.

Thank you for your attention to this matter. I await your response.

Sincerely,

____
    (Signature)
Enclosure

Cease and Desist

Your Name
Address
City, State Zip

Date
Debt Collector's Name
Address
City, State Zip

Re: Account Number (put your account number here)

Dear Debt Collector:

Pursuant to my rights under federal debt collection laws, I am requesting that you cease and desist communication with me, as well as my family and friends, in relation to this and all other alleged debts you claim I owe.

You are hereby notified that if you do not comply with this request, I will immediately file a complaint with the Federal Trade Commission and the [your state here] Attorney General's office. Civil and criminal claims will be pursued.

Sincerely,

Your Name